MW00885167

This Book Belongs To:

____

Made in United States
North Haven, CT
04 June 2023

37341776R00063